# Hajj
# Stories

Published by Evans Brothers Ltd
2A Portman Mansions
Chiltern St
London W1U 6NR

First published 2005

The text of *Hajj Stories* is based on *The Story of Hajar* and *The Story of Ibrahim and Ismail*, two stories originally published in Islamic Stories, a title in the Storyteller series published by Evans Brothers Ltd.

British Library Cataloguing in Publication Data
Ganeri, Anita
    Festival stories: the Hajj story
    1. Muslim pilgrims and pilgrimages – Saudi
Arabia – Mecca – Juvenile literature
    I. Title
    297. 3'52

ISBN 0 237 52732 4

Printed in China by WKT Company Limited

Editor: Julia Bird
Designer: Robert Walster
Illustrations: Tracy Fennell
Production: Jenny Mulvanny
Consultant: Toby Mayer

Acknowledgements:
For permission to reproduce copyright material, the author and publishers gratefully acknowledge the following:
Page 7 Art Director's and Trip Photo Library
Page 21 Art Director's and Trip Photo Library

**A note on the illustrations in this book**

*Throughout this book, patterns have been used to decorate the pages rather than pictures of people or animals. This is because Muslims traditionally believe that human beings and animals can only be created by Allah, not by human artists.*

# Hajj
# Stories

Anita Ganeri

Illustrated by
Tracy Fennell

Evans

# Contents

# THE HAJJ PILGRIMAGE

The Hajj is a special journey, or pilgrimage, which all Muslims try to make at least once in their lives. They travel to the holy city of Makkah, in Saudi Arabia, where the Prophet Muhammad (peace and blessings be upon him) was born in 570 CE. Muhammad was the last and greatest of the prophets, or messengers, sent by Allah to teach people about Islam. When they arrive in Makkah, the pilgrims change into simple, white clothes to show that everyone is equal.

Then they visit holy sites in and around Makkah. The Hajj begins at the cube-shaped Ka'bah. The pilgrims walk around the Ka'bah seven times. Then they walk or run between two small hills to remember the story of Hajar, the wife of the Prophet Ibrahim. Later, at a place called Mina, they throw stones at three stone pillars which stand for the devil. This reminds them of the story of Ibrahim and his son, Isma'il. Finally, the pilgrims return to the Ka'bah and walk around it seven more times.

# THE STORY OF HAJAR

The Prophet Ibrahim (peace be upon him) lived peacefully with his two wives, Sara and Hajar, and his young son, Isma'il, whom he loved very much. Although he was a wealthy man, he was also very humble and devout. In fact, he was so holy that he was called the Friend of Allah. He spent his life praising Allah and living as Allah wanted him to.

The Holy Qur'an tells this story about Ibrahim, Isma'il and Hajar. Once, a very long time ago, Ibrahim had a dream. He dreamt that Allah was speaking to him. Allah told him to take Hajar and Isma'il into the desert and to leave them there. Ibrahim did not have to think twice. As always, he was ready to obey Allah's commands.

When Ibrahim told Hajar where they were going, she was very frightened. But she followed Ibrahim into the desert, carrying Isma'il in her arms.

"Why are you doing this?" she asked her husband.

"Because Allah wishes me to," Ibrahim replied. "And I have promised to do whatever Allah commands."

Then Ibrahim walked away, leaving Hajar and Isma'il alone in the desert.

It was the hottest time of the day. The Sun was high in the sky, and the desert was baking hot. But wherever Hajar looked, there was no shade to be found.

Hajar had brought some dates and water with her, but they soon ran out. Hajar and Isma'il were very thirsty. But where could Hajar find water in the middle of the desert?

Everywhere Hajar looked was dry and dusty. But perhaps there would be water in the hills nearby? So Hajar left Isma'il and walked from one hill to the other. Back and forth she went, but no water could she find. Whatever would they do?

Then Hajar heard a voice calling to her, and she saw the angel, Jibril, standing close by. The angel was pointing at Isma'il.

Suddenly, Hajar saw water springing up from the ground around Isma'il's feet. There was all the water she and Isma'il could possibly drink. All the time, Allah had been watching over them and now he had saved them from harm.

From then on, this spring became known as the sacred Well of Zamzam, and its fame spread far and wide.

# THE STORY OF IBRAHIM AND ISMA'IL

The Holy Qur'an tells another story about the Prophet Ibrahim.

One night, Ibrahim had another dream. In this dream, Allah spoke to him once more and gave him another command. He told Ibrahim to sacrifice the most precious person in his life – his beloved son, Isma'il. Ibrahim was very sad. Isma'il was only ten years old. Why would Allah want Ibrahim to kill him?

But Ibrahim had dedicated his whole life to obeying Allah. So he went to find Isma'il and told him about his dream.

"Don't be sad, father," Isma'il said. "We must follow Allah's wishes and do what he wants us to do."

So Ibrahim took Isma'il to Mina, a place close to the holy city of Makkah. This is where he would carry out Allah's wishes and sacrifice Isma'il, his son.

On the way to Mina, their path was blocked by a sinister stranger. It was the devil in disguise.

"Where are you going?" asked the stranger.

"I am going to Mina to carry out Allah's wishes," Ibrahim replied.

"But surely Allah is good and kind?" said the stranger. "He would not want you to kill your son. That must be the work of the devil. Go home and forget all about it."

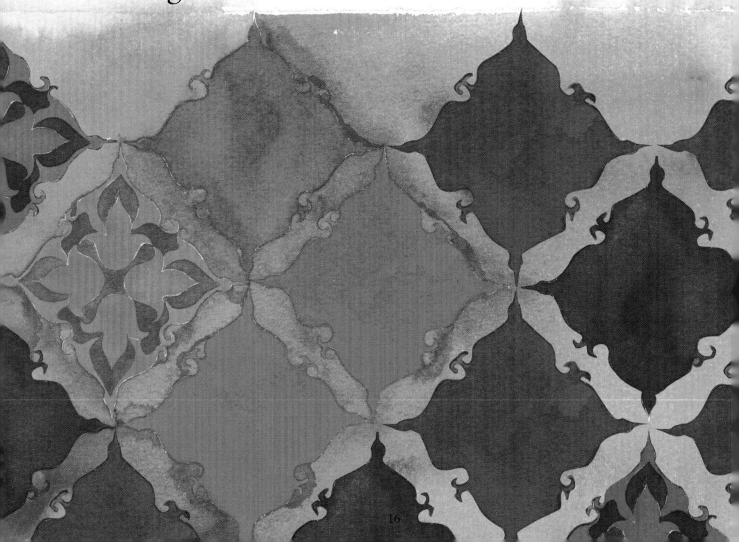

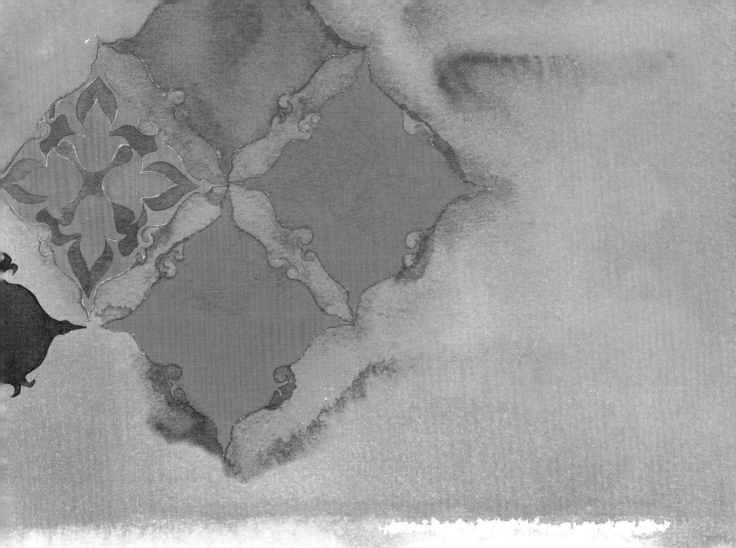

Then Ibrahim recognised the stranger and saw that it was the devil himself. Ibrahim did not listen to what he said, but carried on on his way. But the devil did not give up. Next, he turned to Isma'il.

"Did you know," he asked the boy, "that your father is planning to kill you? What do you think of that, boy?"

"He must do as Allah commands," replied Isma'il, calmly.

Still the devil did not give up. He went to see Hajar, Isma'il's mother, and told her what Ibrahim was planning to do. But, like Ibrahim and Isma'il, Hajar would not listen.

"He must do as Allah commands," she said.

Then Ibrahim and Isma'il each picked up a handful of stones. They threw them at the devil to drive him away.

Now the time had come for the greatest test. It was time for Ibrahim to kill his son as a sacrifice to Allah. Isma'il lay down on the ground. Then Ibrahim picked up his knife.

"I am sorry, my dear son," he said. "But I must follow Allah's commands, even in this."

But, just as he was about to kill Isma'il, the knife was twisted out of his hand.

Ibrahim looked around him but he could not see anyone. Then he heard Allah's voice calling to him.

"Oh, Ibrahim," the voice said. "Do not hurt Isma'il. You were willing to obey me, even if it meant killing your son. Kill this ram instead."

So Ibrahim and Isma'il caught the ram which Allah had sent and sacrificed it instead, just as Allah had commanded.

# ID-UL-ADHA

At the end of the Hajj, Muslims all over the world remember the story of Ibrahim and Isma'il by celebrating the festival of Id-ul-Adha. Early on Id morning, Muslims dress in their best clothes and go to the mosque for prayers. After the prayers, the imam gives a talk about the importance of the festival. Then, to remind people of Ibrahim's sacrifice, a sheep or goat is killed. Some meat is shared out among friends, family and the poor. People also exchange gifts of sweets and Id cards.

# An Id Prayer

This is a prayer which Muslims recite on Id day to praise Allah. It is said in the Arabic language, but an English translation is given here.

'Allah is great, Allah is great,
Allah is great.
There is no god but Allah.
Allah is great, Allah is great.
To Him all praise belongs.
Allah is the greatest,
All praise belongs to Him.
And glory to Allah,
In the evening and in the morning.
There is no god but Allah, the Unique.'

# Making an Id sweet box

At Id-ul-Adha, many Muslims give presents to their friends and family. A popular present is a box of delicious sweets, made from nuts, dates and honey. Try making your own box of sweets to give to a friend.

**You will need:**

a sheet of thin card (plain or coloured)

coloured paper or felt-tip pens

safe scissors

glue

paper clips

paper fasteners

tissue paper

## What to do:

1. Copy the template on to the card and cut the shape out.
You can make it as big or small as you like, but make sure the
template shape stays the same.

2. Fold the card along the dotted lines.

3. Glue the outside of the tabs (marked A, B, C and D) to the inside of
the sides of the box. Hold them in place with paper clips, while the
glue dries.

4. Decorate the box with pieces of coloured paper, or felt-tip pens,
using some of the patterns inside this book.

5. Copy the handle on to card. Cut it out and decorate it.

6. Fix the ends of the handle to the ends of the box, using glue or
paper fasteners.

7. Put some crumpled-up
tissue paper in the box and
fill it with sweets.

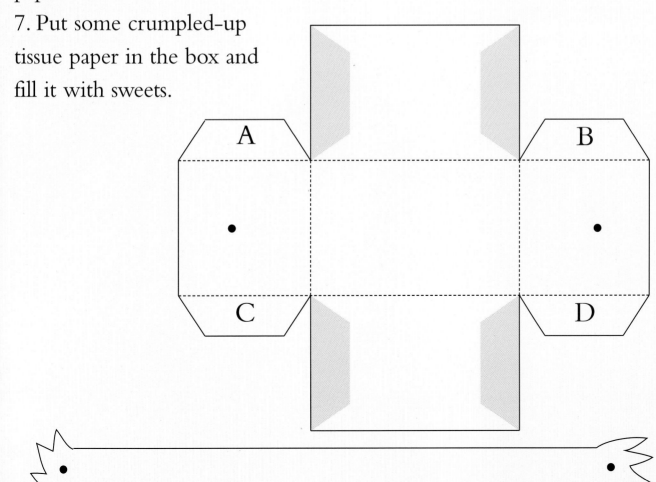

## If you enjoyed this book,
## why not read another book in this series?

*The Christmas Story (pbk)*            0 237 52468 6
*The Christmas Story Big Book*     0 237 52359 0

*The Divali Story (pbk)*                0 237 52471 6
*The Divali Story Big Book*        0 237 52469 4

*The Easter Story (pbk)*                0 237 52475 9
*The Easter Story Big Book*        0 237 52470 8

*The Hanukkah Story (pbk)*         0 237 52653 0
*The Hanukkah Story Big Book*    0 237 52652 2

*The Passover Story (pbk)*          0 237 52655 7
*The Passover Story Big Book*     0 237 52654 9